Ways to Go

TRUCKS GO!

By Sean MacDumont

Gareth Stevens
PUBLISHING

Please visit our website, www.garethstevens.com. For a free color catalog of all our high-quality books, call toll free 1-800-542-2595 or fax 1-877-542-2596.

Cataloging-in-Publication Data

Names: MacDumont, Sean.
Title: Trucks go! / Sean MacDumont.
Description: New York : Gareth Stevens Publishing, 2018. | Series: Ways to go | Includes index.
Identifiers: ISBN 9781538210291 (pbk.) | ISBN 9781538210307 (library bound) | ISBN 9781538208472 (6 pack)
Subjects: LCSH: Trucks–Juvenile literature.
Classification: LCC TL230.15 M33 2018 | DDC 629.224–dc23

First Edition

Published in 2018 by
Gareth Stevens Publishing
111 East 14th Street, Suite 349
New York, NY 10003

Editor: Kate Mikoley
Designer: Sam DeMartin

Photo credits: Cover, p. 1 Art Konovalov/Shutterstock.com; pp. 5, 24 (semi) Henryk Sadura/Shutterstock.com; p. 7 Rainer Plendl/Shutterstock.com; p. 9 James Steidl/Shutterstock.com; p. 11 oksana.perkins/Shutterstock.com; pp. 13, 24 (highway) Natalia Bratslavsky/Shutterstock.com; p. 15 rCarner/Shutterstock.com; pp. 17, 24 (wheel) Maksim Shmeljov/Shutterstock.com; p. 19 Lopolo/Shutterstock.com; p. 21 J.D. Maman/Shutterstock.com; p. 23 Mike Kuhlman/Shutterstock.com.

Printed in the United States of America

CPSIA compliance information: Batch #CW18GS: For further information contact Gareth Stevens, New York, New York at 1-800-542-2595.

Contents

Trucks go far!

Big trucks are
called semis.

3000R

Some have 18 wheels!

Some weigh 40 tons!

They go on big roads.
These are highways.

Drivers sit in the cab.

Monster trucks go
off the road!

LUCAS OIL
LUCAS OIL
L.A.SUPERTRUX Presents..
BIGFOOT

Fire trucks help put out fires.

10

Some trucks bring
food to stores.

he quality food people

Some trucks even carry cars!

Words to Know

highway

semi

wheel

Index